RHUBARB

BY JANET BARNES
ILLUSTRATED BY RANIE KEITHAHN

Thanks to Sue Platt for the author photo.

ISBN: 978-1-943258-77-2

🦉 **Warren** publishing

Published by WARREN Publishing
Charlotte, NC
www.warrenpublishing.net
Printed in the United States

This book is dedicated to Kyle and Colin,
my grandsons who have grown up so fast,
especially Colin who encouraged me to make it rhyme.
To the towns throughout the country that
grow and celebrate rhubarb.
And of course to Bev and her rhubarb!

There once was a lady
so special and kind,
you could search the world over
and still never find
anyone kinder than Bev.

Now Bev loved to garden and
grew fruits and veggies galore,
that she cooked in her kitchen
making food you'd adore!

She invited her friends
to share what she had,
and if you couldn't make it,
you felt really bad.

You wouldn't want to miss the pie
made from something
she grew in her garden …
RHUBARB!
Now there's a surprise.

Bev's **FIRST** garden was in Alaska,
which is far to the north.
It's so far north that in winter
it can be dark all day, and in summer
the daylight never goes away!

The darkness makes it hard to grow things.
Plants need both light and dark,
but when you do your very best
and try especially hard …

anything is possible,
and Bev didn't quit.
She grew flowers and tomatoes,
blueberries too,
lettuce and radishes,
but let me tell you …

the thing that grew best of all was …

RHUBARB!

Bev's **SECOND** garden
was on an island in Washington state,
where summer was warmer
but sometimes came late.

The weather was milder
with sunshine and showers …

but deer brought their babies
and ate all her flowers!

And radishes …
and blueberries!

So Bev took a ferry
and went into town
where she bought
a tall fence that
she put all around.

Soon she had veggies
that she'd grown and
not bought,

beetroot
and cauliflower …

string beans and peas,
tomatoes, blueberries,
and apples on trees.

But the plant that came from
Alaska was the biggest of all.

Can you guess what it was?
RHUBARB, of course!

Bev's **THIRD** garden
was special because
it was on the shore.
All her favorite things grew there,
but there was so much more.

There were quail,
funny birds with squiggles on their heads,
and little, tiny oysters hiding in their beds.

Eagles flew overhead.
Fish swam in the stream.
There were fruits on the trees,
it was just like a dream.

She grew roses and marigolds
that trailed down the stairs …

three kinds of apples,

and two kinds of pears …

… raspberries,
strawberries,
lettuce too!

But you know what grew
best of all, don't you?

RHUBARB, of course!

Now that you know about rhubarb,
I have a surprise for you!
All over America
(and some other countries too!)
people like it so much,
they have "Rhubarb Day"
with festivals, parades, food,
and lots of games to play.

MAYBE YOU CAN FIND ONE SOMEWHERE NEAR YOU!

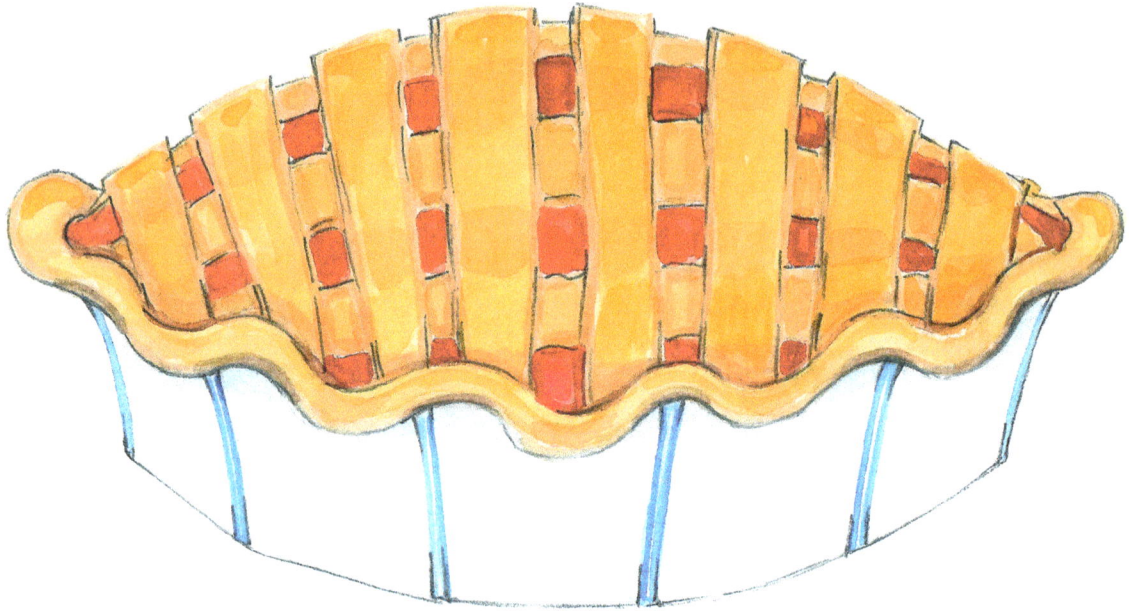

Rhubarb Orange Pie

1 ³/₄ c. sugar (plus a little extra for top crust)
9" pie shells for top and bottom
6 Tbsp. flour
4 c. rhubarb (cut into ¹/₂" lengths)
1 ¹/₃ Tbsp. butter
1 orange (chunked)
1 egg, beaten

Mix flour and sugar, add rhubarb, chunked up orange, and beaten egg.
Pour in pastry shell.
Dot with butter. Cover with top crust. Sprinkle with sugar.
Bake 425° for 40-50 minutes (put foil under pie pan to catch drips).